visit to the POLICE STATION

CHILDRENS PRESS®

CHICAGO

by Dotti Hannum
photos by Romie Flanagan

With appreciation to the City of Evanston, Illinois, Police Department and to Chief of Police, William H. Logan, for their cooperation in the photographing of this book.

And to the children who worked with us so patiently as we recorded their visit to the police station on film.

Library of Congress Cataloging in Publication Data

Hannum, Dotti.
  A visit to the police station.

  (Field trip series)
  Summary: Describes the activities that take place at a police station and the various duties of the police men and women.
  1. Police—Juvenile literature.   [1. Police]
I. Flanagan, Romie, ill.   II. Title.   III. Series.
HV7922.H28   1985   363.2   84-12700
ISBN 0-516-01493-5

2 3 4 5 6 7 8 9 10 11 12 R 92 91 90 89 88 87 86

visit to the POLICE STATION

Created by The Child's World

Mr. Vargas holds the door open. His
class walks inside. They are visiting a police station.

Mr. Vargas talks with a policeman at a desk.

"Your guide today will be Officer Briggs," the policeman says. "He will be here shortly."

Officer Briggs waves to the class. "Welcome to the police station, boys and girls," he says. "Stay together. And follow me." He leads the way.

At the Communications Center, the class looks inside. Someone is always busy here. This is where all police calls are answered.

"See the lights," says Officer Briggs.
"The red lights show which police officers
are already busy. The green lights show
which ones are free."

"Why?" asks Jim.

"Someone in the city may need help,"
says Officer Briggs. "We can see at once
which police officers are free and in the
area. They can answer the call quickly."

"Why do they have a TV in the Communications Center?" asks Tony.

"To watch what is happening in other parts of the police station. Sometimes those we arrest start trouble. Someone here can watch and send help," says Officer Briggs.

"Officer Jones," he says, "is talking to someone who has a CB radio. Someone here listens for radio calls all the time. "Now let's visit the prisoner dock."

"We bring people in here in a police car," he continues. "We shut this door. Then we let the prisoners out of the car. That's so they can't run away." Officer Briggs opens the door. The class goes outside.

Outside, Officer Briggs leads the children to a van. "I'll open the door. You can see the long seats on each side," he says. "A prisoner could never hide anything in this van.

"Now let's see a squad car," says Officer Briggs. "Officer Castella will show us."

"Turn on the siren!" says Andrew. But
first Officer Castella turns on the flashing
red lights. And he turns on the white side
lights, called alley lights.

Finally, he turns on the bright spotlight.
The children stick their fingers in their ears.
And they wait. Here it comes! rrrrrRRRRR-
rrrrr! rrrrrRRRRRrrrrr!

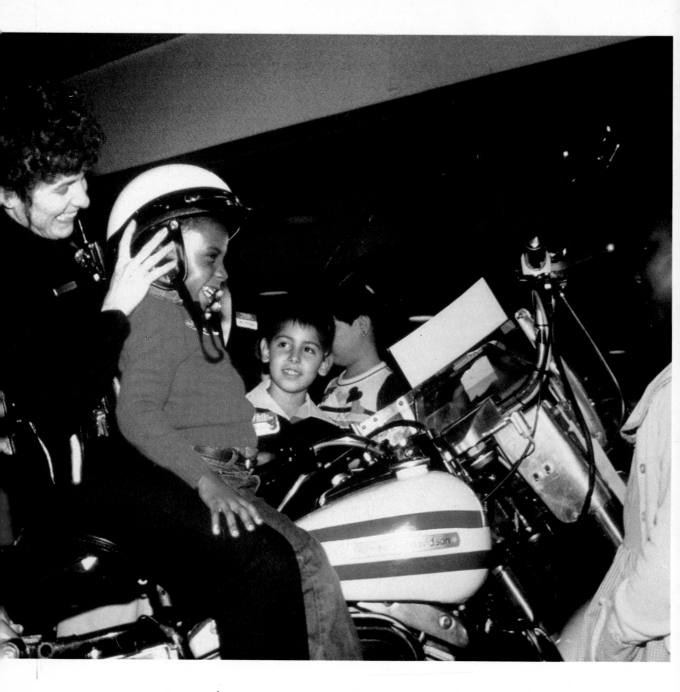

A policewoman rides into the parking garage on a motorcycle. She lets the children look at her bike and beep the horn. Tony even tries on her helmet.

Officer Briggs takes the class back inside. They pass another officer. He has a
police dog with him.

"Do you have a police dog?" Maria
asks.

"No," says Officer Briggs. "But several
officers here do. A police officer and his
dog are a team."

"We must hurry on," says Officer Briggs.
But he stops to show the children a "most-
wanted" poster.

The class walks past Officer Castella. He
is working on his report. "A police officer
has to do a lot of writing," he says. "I'm
glad I learned how to spell."

The next stop is the shooting range. "Here police officers shoot at targets," says Officer Briggs. "Sometimes they turn out the bright lights. They practice with only red lights on. That helps them learn how to shoot at night."

Officer Briggs puts earmuffs on some of
the children. He tells the children that police officers wear earmuffs when they
practice shooting. That keeps the sound
from hurting their ears.

Next the class goes to the Booking Room. That's where police officers first take prisoners they arrest. Officer Briggs holds up an envelope. "When we arrest someone," he says, "we put his money, keys, rings, and things in an envelope. We put them away. We keep them for him.

"Then we make fingerprints," he adds.
"Everyone's fingerprints are different."
The children learn how a fingerprint is
made.

Jim climbs up on a stool. "Let's pretend we are taking his mug shot," says Officer Briggs. He shows the children how a prisoner is given a number.

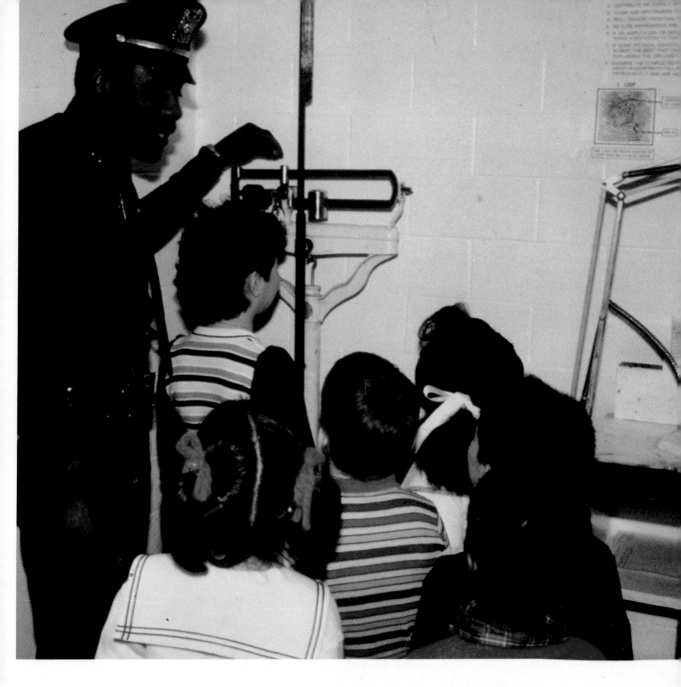

A scale is in the room. Leanne steps on it. "I'll weigh you," says Officer Briggs. Next he measures Andrew. The police weigh and measure those they arrest. Then they put them in a jail cell.

Finally the children get to the jail cells. Inside each cell is a bed and a toilet. "We give a prisoner only a blanket," says Officer Briggs.

"The bed looks hard," says Leanne.
Tony agrees.

Next Officer Briggs shows them the key
to the cell door. Leanne tries it. It works.

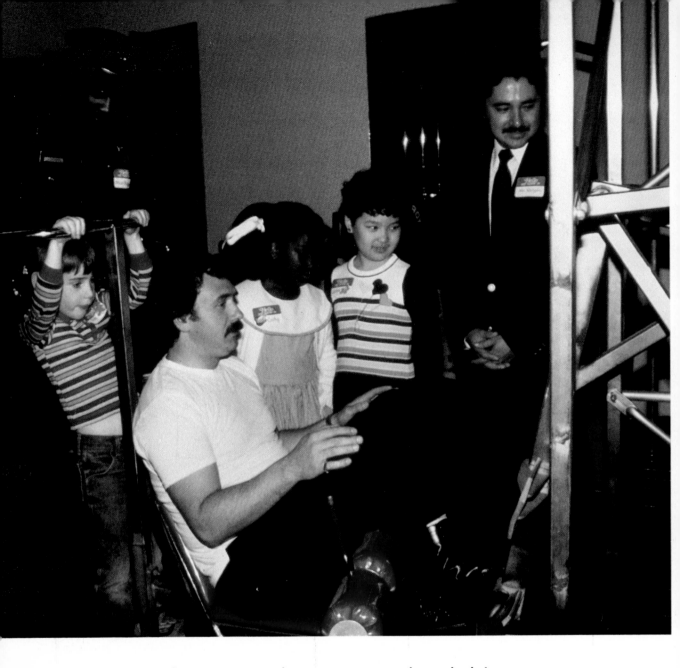

The visit is almost over. The children stop in the exercise room. A policeman is doing his exercises. Police officers need to keep in shape.

Then Officer Briggs introduces the class to Officer Friendly.

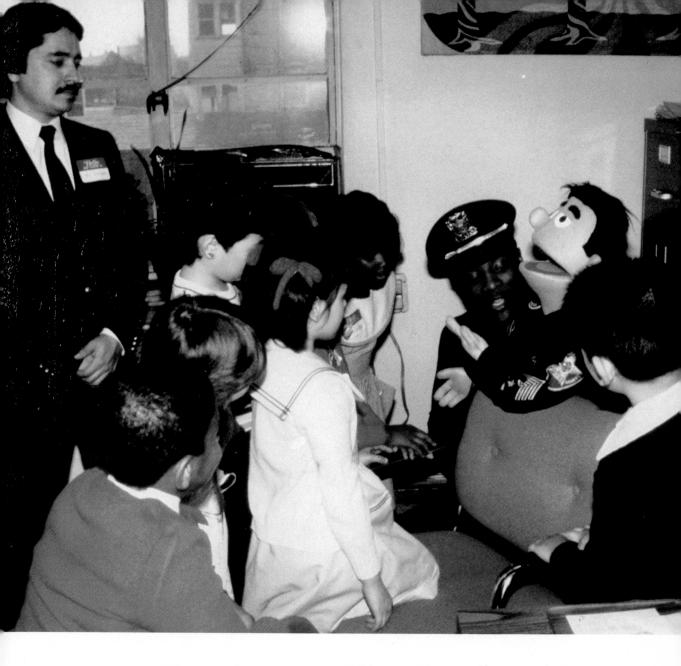

"Someday soon, Officer Friendly and I will come and visit your school," says Officer Briggs. "We will talk about bicycles and safety. Do you have licenses for your bicycles?"

"No," say several children.

"If someone should steal your bicycle, you would wish it had a license number," says Officer Briggs. "Police put license numbers of stolen bikes into computers. Then if a bike is found, it can be given back to its owner." The children like that idea a lot.

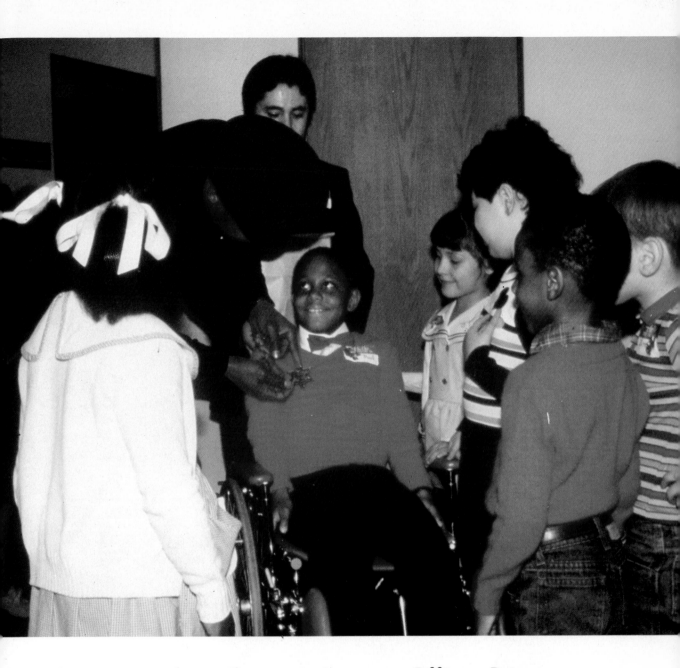

At last, the visit is over. Officer Briggs
pins a special police badge on each child.
"When someone asks where you got
this, won't you have a lot of things to tell?"
he says.